Domestic Violence

The Cure

By

Benjamin Janey

Prevention – Intervention - Redemption

Published by Ben Official Books

ISBN-10: 0615838952

ISBN-13: 978-0615838953

Library of Congress Control Number: 2013911577

First Edition, June 2013

Printed in the United States of America

Publisher's Note

"Never value a book based on page count because the content is what you'll find as priceless." –Ben Official Books

Cover concept by: Shane Cox

Edited by: Benjamin Janey

Graphic Designer: RIP Graphics LLC

Ben Official Books www.benofficialbooks.com

Dedication

This book is dedicated to Donna Janey and all who would like to make this world a better place by realizing, "We cannot change our ways until we change our minds."

Introduction

Domestic violence has been increasing, regardless of nationwide polls and pacifying statistics. Some may not report the abuse, and a disproportionate number of victims are depending upon a "Restraining Order" to elucidate such an undetected form of mental illness.

In this Workbook, you and I will take on this mental illness like never before. Contrary to the traditional analysis and conception that incline to see it as just a problem, there's more. I've been in domestic violence programs that are effective only on paper and while in class. Consequently, intervention can no longer be the brightest idea when there's an imperative prognosis. We'd like to believe that by discussing what has occurred will change things. Until now, here's a mental illness that must be dealt with by going to the root.

One might ask, "What is the root?" Is it not: Keeping our hands to ourselves, how to disagree, how to talk to one another, and knowing how to love one another?

Well, that has been the focus and could only be the "solution" if we continue to ascertain that domestic violence is just a problem and not a form of mental illness. An illness has to be diagnosed, a cure found, and the afflicted treated. A solution in this instance would only pave part of the way. The lettered man has a book sense and great dialogue regarding the subject matter. However, without further delay, I present to you The Cure.

The typical Power and Control Wheel skims across the surface and truly identifies what takes place in a domestic violence situation; a great tool for intervention. Nonetheless, I'd like to reintroduce Prevention, Intervention, and Redemption like never before. With that being said, if an abuser's behavior clearly shows that they have lost their mind, due to committing acts of senseless behavior, aka gone crazy, then it is what it is.

During a domestic violence episode, looking from the outside in, we'd be quick to say, "He or she is crazy for doing that!" When the heat is on, there's no time to be politically correct. Although, we know the correct terminology to use are the safe words like: insane or mentally ill. But, let's deal with crazy today.

The main premise and conclusion has been that someone has a problem with their hands, and we hit to solve our problems. Be that as it may, keep in mind that we are no longer dealing with just a problem.

We've assumed that due to a person's childhood, they've seen abuse in their homes and acquired bad habits. The abuser blames it on anger, alcohol, and drugs. Some victims see themselves at fault.

It's in our social arenas two fold. Quite the norm in the urban setting, "The Man" supposedly runs the relationship and has a so-called right to put a woman "In her place." This is done without a care in the world, in public or private because he wants to be heard, recognized, and respected! Whereas, in the suburbs others will handle the same situation behind closed doors to uphold their appearances in the community. They care about what their neighbors and others may think of them.

Primarily, I am dealing with men abusing women because this is the subject I know. However, women abusing men and same sex relationships are covered as well. Ironically, it just depends on what role is applicable, be it victim or abuser. Certain things are gender base, yet as I began to expound on the subject, I realized many victims and abusers share commonality to a significant degree.

The victims may blame themselves by rationalizing, irrationally. "Well, if I wouldn't have said this nor done that, it would have never happened."

Stop right there! Whatever a person chooses to do or say is their birth right called FREE WILL. Regardless, if it's a relationship or marriage – there's no ownership!

The abuser would agree with their victim being at fault, becoming apologetic for their abusive behavior. By showing temporary affection they are only pacifying the matter, until next time. Did you know that some people think that make up sex is the best sex and is a means to an end?

The illness is with the abuser and they don't realize that they are sick. Our polite society has pointed out that "the abuser" needs counseling or "the victim and abuser" both need counseling. In any event, an admission of guilt, within a fixed amount of time for counseling, doesn't make it all better nor go away simply by discussing what has occurred.

At what rate could we convince the victim who's been beat for years that it gets better? What about those whose restraining orders have been violated on numerous occasions; the parents, families, and friends who had to bury their child or loved one? Unfortunately, a band aid is not a cure!

What makes what I have to say any different and who made me an expert in such a field, you're probably wondering?

Life has a lesson and once learned must be taught to others. My past experiences and the shameful things that I've done forced me to help myself change. Someone has to draw the line in the sand because if we knew better, we'd do better.

One thing for certain, there's a cycle. No matter the method of therapy, until we face the facts and go to the root, we'll continue going in circles. But how deep is this root?

The Victim is faced with:

1. Verbal Abuse – That's the yelling and screaming. The mental breakdown of their self esteem inflicted upon them by the abuser. This creates the fear factor.
2. Physical Abuse – This is when the hitting, controlling and damaging of person; even personal property starts.
3. Mental Abuse - This is when the abuser soothes the victim's mind with promise, apology after apology.
4. The Repeat- The above doesn't stop rearing its ugly head until we examine the point of origin, take preventive measures, intervene, and prescribe the daily treatment for the abuser to cure themselves.

The Cure is correcting the thought process as to WHY someone is an Abuser:

1. Mental – The Abuser has to get his/her mind right.
2. Physical - The Abuser has to keep his/her hands to themselves, and learn where they need to apply themselves in the relationship or marriage besides the bedroom.

3. Verbal - The Abuser has to say what he/she means and mean what he/she says. However, he/she must choose his/her words and tone correctly. Under no circumstances does the language or tone suppose to bring love to a standstill or create road blocks; thinking before speaking.

4. The Cure- This may sound too simple to believe: Apply daily the forthcoming information!

Allow me to walk you through real life. There are no warning signs in advance or posted on someone's forehead stating, "I tend to get abusive!" There are no excuses about pushing someone's buttons or being rubbed the wrong way. This approach is not for you to try and help someone else. They have to help themselves by first realizing why they have issues.

Chapter One-Prevention

Are we beginning from a position of strength or weakness?

This is a series of questions that we must ask ourselves when first considering a relationship or starting over.

1. Why do we want a relationship?
2. Are we ready to give up or compromise the freedom of being single?
3. Do we have time to share our lives right now or do we already find ourselves with not enough hours in a day?
4. Are we allowing sexual/physical attraction to outweigh logical reasoning when choosing a mate?
5. Are we confusing a bed mate with a soul mate?
6. Do we have realistic goals that we haven't met yet? Such as: our own place to live, a car, and employment?
7. Are we willing to share our place, car, and pay check just for the sake of saying that you have a man or woman?
8. Do we inspect what we expect?
   a. Can he/she read?
   b. Who's their family and friends?
   c. Do they have a place, a car and visible employment?
   d. Would we accept a weed smoker, drinker or casual drug user?
9. Do they belong to a church, temple, synagogue, or even have a religion?
10. Has either of us been tested for HIV/AIDS?
11. Or will it be: because we're lonely, horny and they look good, we'll just "hope" things work out?

Why do we want a relationship?

Relationships seem to be a natural desire. We've seen some shape or form of it in our homes. In our youth, we begin friendships and become selective of our playmates. On television, we've seen dating and married couples of the opposite sex, and in modern times even same sex relationships. With all of this going on around us, one day we find ourselves liking someone.

Growing up, like and love goes hand in hand. When we like someone and we're liked in return, it's misconstrued as love. There is a great feeling of looking forward to someone's presence. There's a void being met, a safety and comfort, because we've found someone that understands and appreciates us. They want to be with us and we want to be with them, and that's all that matters. The spell has been cast; cupid has shot his arrow.

Many might recall the love notes and messages being passed in school: Do you like me, yes or no? A friend telling us that, "So and so said they like us!" Sharing is caring in our youthful days; be it lunch, crayons, toys, candy, or Valentine's Day cards, we are officially on our way.

There was nothing better than eating, sleeping, and dreaming of a person. Of course, this was a typical pattern, being that our immediate peers, siblings, and family members were going through it as well. Emulating behavior is an adaptation of our surroundings.

How do we know what's a good relationship? Is it based on what we've seen and what we've heard? The answer to this is, absolutely!

One of the first things we pick up on is possessiveness. If so and so like us and we like them, then neither one of us can like someone else. The consequence of this is: we develop a mind state that we have every right to claim ownership of a person.

With all of that being said, the question still remains: Why do we want a relationship? Well…because everyone else has one.

Are we ready to give up or compromise the freedom of being single?

When we are very young there's really no say so in how we spend our time. Our parents or guardians normally have that mapped out for us. Yet, in our teenage years we are gradually given the freedom to make our own decisions.

We independently begin by going to the movies, school dances, parks or our friends' homes. We cannot live without a phone. Nowadays, a cell phone is like a body part to most of us. All of this changes the level and practice of how we like someone. Our playmates become BFF's and our bonds become stronger. Meanwhile, the demands and rules within a relationship change dramatically. There are no longer child-like expectations and possessiveness gives both parties an inquiring mind.

Take for example: In a teenage relationship, the relationship becomes a questionnaire. Everything we do has to be accounted for. Things such as: Where are we going? When are we going to call them? How come they can't see us? Why don't we have any time for them? Who was that we were talking too, and why didn't we answer our phones? Now these are just a few things that we crowd one another with. Here it is, our parents or guardians have finally given us freedom. Yet, guilty are we for already trying to take it away from one another in the name of love.

Our friends and siblings also have an opinionated say in what goes on in our lives. Everyone expects our time to be shared with them like it use to be. Is there "Me" time? This is the time we begin to wish we had for ourselves. Eventually, with family and friends constantly in your ear, having a relationship may not seem like the best idea after all. Being young or no longer tied down, having yet to explore the free world makes us curious about many things. The monotonous   pressure interferes with what we have in mind for ourselves. This makes or may cause our first break up to be inevitable. Chances are we'll begin to subconsciously build resentment. This regret can be due to the fact that we're caught in a tug of war for our time by others.

Once we begin or are now starting over we develop our own thoughts. Our likes and dislikes quickly prove that apparently having a serious relationship is no longer major. We are just beginning to find ourselves. At this point, fun takes on a greater priority rather than being tied down. We can now meet new people, enjoy new conversation and remain casual with no need for a commitment. The checks and balances that we longed for in a relationship didn't add up and being free seems to be the way to go. That is until our fondness of someone or their fondness of us takes us down that road again.

Yes, those were the good old days. Remember talking on the phone to someone until one of us fell asleep? How about writing both of our names inside of a heart or kissing a picture and telling the person in the picture we love them? This could have occurred weekly, monthly or lasted longer. But, at some point in our lives it did occur.

As adults, or rebounding, the bar of expectations has been raised. Each of us now has a definite expectation as to what is the right type of relationship for us. We have it going on now. We have accomplished a few things in life. We have plans and a vision of how to see things through. We have a schedule and set way of how we do things. We also find ourselves in love again.

Do we have time to share our lives right now or do we already find ourselves with not enough hours in a day?

Every day is like a new adventure. We try to plan our day accordingly. Yet, most times it's based on someone else's availability. For example, we call our friends to see what time they are going to be ready. We may be borrowing the family car or picking someone up and need to know a time. We may be scheduled to work or attend class at a set time. So often, there's so much we'd like to do in a day that we just can't find the time to squeeze it all in. In the real world, something always comes up.

Day in and day out, this is just us trying to manage the hustle and bustle in our own lives, never mind in a relationship. Realistically, if we don't have time for ourselves, "Do we think that we have time for a relationship or marriage?"

Are we allowing sexual/physical attraction to outweigh logical reasoning when choosing a mate?

We may not be chemists, but swear we can interpret body chemistry. What we see often determines what we like. The apple of our eye just may have a worm inside, and even eye candy can give us a tooth ache.

Are we confusing a bed mate with a soul mate?

At this stage in our lives we've noticed some intriguing things about ourselves. Certain parts of our body respond to certain things. Whether it's the mental thought or physical touch that gets us sexually aroused; it's something that we don't mind feeling.

Dating is the proper formality of executing our plans. We have spotted the apple of our eye. Most of us know from the start what we would do or wouldn't do sexually with a person. It's just a matter of "how" we're going to do this? While we're getting to know one another there's a mental game that must transpire.

Many have a time frame before it's appropriate or justifiable to sleep with someone. In the beginning, nothing could be better. The majority of the time, all of us are on our best behavior. Secretly, we both just might share the same intentions. Sex becomes the weapon and it's just a matter of who's going to pull the trigger first.

The interest that has been shown to us has become everything we'd ever imagined. They could possible do no wrong in our book. The way they look at, hold, and kiss us is all too deserving of something more. The time has come. Now we're willing; hoping that they are able.

At this stage, we are in the heat of the moment. Our vision becomes blurry because we can't see pass that moment. Yes, we'd love these feelings and precious moments to last a lifetime. However, it has slipped our minds completely in regards to, what type of future could the both of us have together? Or even, could there be a future between the both of us?

Without consideration, many relationships are dragged out due to the adverse effects of sexual intercourse. No one gets pregnant by their lonesome. The thought never occurred to either of us, "Are we qualified to become parents and soul mates?"

Wait a minute! Did we just have to think about someone being our soul mate? We are way too young, or have been tied down too long, to be settling down! We still have college, a career, a newfound breath of fresh air, and our entire lives ahead of us! This isn't right! Something is wrong with this picture!

Do we have realistic goals not met yet, such as our own place to live, a car and employment?

We are finally adults or free to live our lives again. We've been anticipating this for years, or while trapped in a bad situation, to move out or be on our own. We've been secretly talking about it amongst friends and family for the longest. Some of us may even have a strategy to make this long awaited dream a reality.

Many go off to college and live on campus just for the experience. Others may have been working and plan to split the cost of an apartment with a friend for starters. Some may have the liberty to live at home, or back at home, and still enjoy the freedoms of being an adult. All and all, these are rites of passage or recourse that we celebrate.

We begin to stay out late just because we can. Purchases are made large and small based on our own decision. Steps are being taken toward our personal goals and achieved because these are the things we set for ourselves. We have developed independence or strive prepensely to regain it.

Are we willing to share our place, car, and pay check just for the sake of saying that you have a man or woman?

Let's just say we're now in a relationship. We decide to invite our "friend" over for dinner and a movie. We're both young or "it's been quite some time" and have raging hormones whenever the two of us are around one another.

Since we have our own place, or we're sharing a place with a roommate, after the movie we decide to further our hospitalities to the bedroom. After it goes down, we both fall asleep in each other's warm embrace.

This becomes routine and we're caught up in the moment. Hypothetically, at present, they're between jobs and would like to go apply for a few jobs that are not on the bus line. Being that we have to work during the day, would we mind if they borrowed our car to go look for a work?

Now of course, we wouldn't want nothing to disturb the groove we've been having lately. So, we agree to let them borrow our car while we're at work. Now that we've sexually committed ourselves to this person, we truly want the best for them. We were picked up from work on time, but noticed that our car is almost out of gas. Not wanting to impose on them, knowing their financial and job situation, we offer to put more gas in our own car. We even offer them our car the following day so that they can continue their job search.

In the course of more pillow talk, they appreciate our help and assure us that they will repay us once they get back on their feet. This warms us up to such a degree that, on our pay day, we voluntarily give them a few dollars. Is this out of sympathy or are we beginning to pay for happiness?

We have gotten quite accustomed to them being around. It's almost like they live there. They've left a few changes of clothes, and now we couldn't fathom sleeping alone. Our roommate doesn't mind because they're hardly ever home. They are just doing the opposite of us somewhere else.

Being caught up in the moment may last longer than we think. Is this what we really want for ourselves? Behind the abundance of pleasure, eventually heartache and pain will surface. Sex can be a weapon because it can kill our dreams.

Do we inspect what we expect?

We may all have a different version of what leads to the perfect combination. It takes a lifetime to truly know a person because we all change like the weather. But, upon inspection there are telltale signs that will let us know what type of person that we are dealing with. Love is blind though and causes us to wander into a relationship full of assumptions to our bitter surprise.

Based on what we have going on for ourselves, in the long run, are the two of us truly compatible? There are basics and minimums for us to calculate our expectations. A poor choice is ours when hoping for the best is all we have for numbers.

Can they read?

This is important to know. If we plan on being with someone for the long haul, there will come a time when both of us need to read the fine print. The ability to read opens more options for the both of us. Ideally, the better they do, the better we do and vice versa. There is no limit to exploration and discovery when able to read. They can become who they need to be because we now know that they can function in any given setting.

Who's their family and friends?

The fruit doesn't fall too far from the tree. We need to know how they are accustomed to living. Was there abuse in their past? How are they around children? How do they feel about the women or men in their family? Did they witness equality or abuse within their family structure? Did they have a positive male or female figure in their lives?

Birds of a feather flock together. Therefore, we need to know who their friends are. Just as an example: Ladies, if the majority of their friends are drug dealers, more than likely they've sold a few drugs themselves. If the majority of their friends are gay, and they just so happens to stay in the mirror longer than you, more than likely they have tendencies. If they glorify a few of their friends or family members who are in the pimp game, more than likely they don't have that much respect for women also. This list could go on for days.

Men, if the majority of their friends are "Ladies of the night," more than likely they've turned a few corners themselves. If the majority of their friends are lesbian, more than likely there are some secrets that could surface and shatter your dreams or fulfill your fantasy. Both examples are just examples and intended to be nonjudgmental, as far as someone's sexual preference goes. It's just best to know, than to find out.

Do they have a place, a car and visible employment?

From the start, we need to know where they live before we invite them into our homes, especially when children are involved. The safety and protection of our children must remain our top priority. Unfortunately, this may mean remaining single until we are absolutely certain and comfortable with that person. We need to know who they stay with or who stays with them? Nonetheless, are they living or involved with another woman or man. It's about us knowing, "How they are living?"

The car we've seen them driving is it: theirs, a family member's, a friend's or a rental car? If it's theirs or a rental car, we need to know how they are paying for it. We need to know so one day it won't end up being our responsibility. If it's a family member's or friend's car, we may want to know why they don't have their own car yet.

We've noticed that our new mate dresses nice, has a nice car and keeps money in their pocket. Yet, they're available morning, noon and night. So, what we need to know is how do they make their money?

Okay, let's say they're not available during the day and says they work at such and such a place. Did we see them work there? What's their schedule and days off? When are around us, does their phone ring/vibrate a lot? Do they always have to run out real quick and will be right back?

A word to the wise in this scenario would be, "All that glitters might not be gold!" If we're trying to live a certain way, we cannot let love bring us down. A drug dealer may be able to buy us nice things, at the moment. A cheating mate may be able to pleasure us, but only for a time. Within the blink of an eye, without inspecting what's expected can cost us a life time or our lives.

Would we accept a weed smoker, drinker or casual drug user?

They are attractive enough to have caught our eye, but do we mind if they smoke weed? Will their drinking cost us one day? Does popping pills or sniffing a few lines every now and then bother us?

To fulfill our dreams, we must deal with reality to make our dreams a reality. Having someone in our lives that indulges in escaping reality would not compliment our life styles at all.

Do they belong to a church, temple, synagogue, or even have a religion?

Has it dawned on us that in a relationship a person's religion can cause conflict? We need to know do they belong to a church, temple, synagogue, or even have a religion. Their beliefs or lack of beliefs may shatter our every dream as well.

Again hypothetically speaking, let's just say we are accustomed to going to church on Sundays. They never want to accompany us. Our friends and family ask, "Why they don't attend with us?" How about, going to church is against their religion? What if in time, suddenly, they reveal to us all that a lot of things that we do are against their religion?

Are we willing to stop practicing our faith to please them? Are we willing to convert to their religion? How do we deal with our new found love, who out of the blue revealed, they don't believe in God or claim to be a god? All of this is crucial in deciding where should we go from here?

Has either of us been tested for HIV/AIDS?

I know this is a lot to ask, but the life we're trying to save now is our own. We might have been virgins when all of the above began. But, many of us haven't found a smooth way to ask someone the most serious question before sexual intercourse. Has either of us been tested for HIV/AIDS?

Don't be fooled to count out courtship and believe life is by trial and error. Every test in life doesn't come with a study guide, and this is one test that we need to pass. How lightly we value ourselves, living for the moment. There's a process and better way of doing things when realizing the true basics. By reading further and answering the following questions, in our own words, we are making a conscious choice that will help us cure abusive behavior and avoid domestic violence. Or will it be, because we're lonely, horny and they look good, we'll just "hope" things work out. None of us should ever want to be the ones to say, "We told you so."

Chapter One-Prevention - Questions

Are we beginning from a position of strength or weakness?

1. **Why do you want a relationship?**

_____

_____

_____

_____

_____

_____

_____

_____

_____

_____

_____

_____

_____

_____

_____

_____

2. **Are you ready to give up or compromise the freedom of being single?**

_____

_____

_____

_____

_____

_____

_____

_____

_____

_____

3. **Do you have time to share your life right now or do you already find yourself with not enough hours in a day?**

_____

_____

_____

_____

_____

_____

_____

_____

_____

_____

_____

4. **Are you allowing sexual/physical attraction to outweigh logical reasoning when choosing a mate?**

_____

_____

_____

_____

_____

_____

_____

_____

_____

_____

_____

_____

5. **Are you confusing a bed mate with a soul mate?**

_____

_____

_____

_____

_____

_____

_____

_____

_____

6. **Do you have realistic goals that you haven't met yet? Such as your own place to live, a car, and employment?**

_____

_____

_____

_____

_____

_____

_____

_____

_____

_____

_____

7. **Are you willing to share your place, car, and pay check just for the sake of saying that you have a man or woman?**

_____

_____

_____

_____

_____

_____

_____

_____

_____

8. Do you inspect what you expect? _____

   a. Can he/she read? _____

   b. Who's their family and friends?

   _____

   _____

   _____

   _____

   _____

   c. Do they have a place, a car and visible employment?

   _____

   _____

   _____

   _____

   d. Would you accept a weed smoker, drinker or casual drug user?

   _____

   _____

   _____

   _____

9. Do they belong to a church, temple, synagogue, or even have a religion?

   _____

   _____

   _____

10. Has either of you been tested for HIV/AIDS?

_____

_____

_____

11. Have you already begun to rather not just "hope" things work out just because you're lonely, horny and they look good? Why or why not?

_____

_____

_____

_____

_____

_____

_____

_____

_____

_____

_____

_____

_____

_____

_____

_____

_____

_____

Chapter Two

Verbal Abuse – Prevention

We may not be able to see the sign on someone's forehead that reads, "I tend to get abusive!" But we sure as hell can hear it coming. Communication is so vital in a relationship from the very start that we have to listen!

If someone wants us to obey them, don't be surprised when they eventually call us out of our name. A dog obeys and we have a choice to agree or disagree. Nowhere in between the two does anyone have the right to beat us into agreement!

Beating us into agreement doesn't have to be physical contact as of yet. Words may hurt sometime even more. It changes us from being who we are and makes us become someone that we're not.

Our comfort level changes when in their presence. We begin to feel as though we have to walk on egg shells. The conversation that we'd like to have with them is postponed because they prefer to argue instead.

If we do find ourselves not being able to talk to a person, it is best for us to learn sign language and wave to them good bye. Really, it's that serious! We have to cut the cancer off before it spreads and becomes fatal.

Listen for the tone in their voice when they speak to us. Are we constantly asking ourselves, "Why do they have an attitude?" If they make it seem like we're their problem, become their solution and part ways.

If we'd like to discuss future plans, household matters, or point out things we'd like to see different in the relationship, but this causes them to get hell bent out of shape...put our sneakers on! No one knows how short their lives may be; only a fool would stick around and learn that it might be over today!

Here are a few telltale signs to let us know we're in a bad situation or we're the crazy one that has this mental illness:

When we are told what to do and not to do, we're in a bad situation. If we're the ones thinking someone died and left them as our boss, then we're crazy.

If we are being timed and questioned about how long it takes us to get from Point A to Point B, then we're in a bad situation. If we are the ones constantly staring at the clock, then we're crazy.

When we're being convinced that our friends and family don't need to see or hear from us, we're in a bad situation. If we're the ones constantly doing the convincing, then we're crazy.

If it's our money, yet we're being told how to spend it or have to part with it because our mate feels the dying need to manage it for us, then we're in a bad situation. If we're the ones regulating their finances, then we're crazy.

If there's more than one television in the home, and it's a problem for us to go watch a show of our choice on another television, we're in a bad situation. If we're the ones who see this as a problem, "Guess what?" We're crazy.

The above are just a few major things that many may identify with. No one point is greater than the next. Our main focus here is to observe how someone speaks to us. Notice that it reflects on how we'll be treated or treat someone. There is no such argument, mum's the word. I can't stress it enough that no one walks around with a sign on their head that says, "I tend to get abusive!"

An abuser shouldn't be expected to know better because if we knew better we'd do better. When we're sick, there are symptoms that would lean towards the probable illness. However, the same old solutions for domestic violence have evidently been accumulative misdiagnoses.

How can we continue to arrive at the prognosis without understanding and pinpointing the causes? Talking about what has already occurred is like crying over spilled milk. The abuser needs to understand the origin of their abusive thought process and how to rid themselves of it.

Before becoming a victim or coming to the realization that we're being victimized, here are a few things to listen out for:

a) Didn't I tell you/ I thought I told you to
b) What they don't allow their man or woman to do
c) Forcing upon you what they don't like
d) Constantly putting you down
e) Giving you the third degree about everything you say and do
f) Expecting you to ask them for permission or approval to do something
g) Questioning who you're on the phone with
h) When you ask them a question and their response is that they might let you do this or that
i) What they think won't be good for you
j) Yelling, screaming and name calling
k) Threatening to commit bodily harm
l) Using their religious views to infringe upon your free will to justify things

m) Yeah right, I dare you, over my dead body

n) I swear to God if you do

o) Ignore you

p) Responding with whatever as if our actions are subject to their consequences.

Take the time and list below the words or phrases that would make you uncomfortable? Some may be listed in the above, yet why and how would this affect you?

_____

_____

_____

_____

_____

_____

_____

_____

_____

_____

_____

_____

_____

_____

_____

_____

_____

_____

Chapter Three

Physical Abuse - Prevention

Unfortunately, we have assumed all that is needed to know regarding what Physical Abuse is. That's the pushing, smacking, punching and kicking in a relationship or marriage. The ultimate physical abuse is to be murdered or pushed to a mental limit whereas we begin to harm ourselves or commit suicide.

Nonetheless, based on what's been introduced to us thus far in this reading, we now can develop a trained ear and have begun to know what to listen for. Normally, an abuser won't physically strike out without broadcasting an alternative. This would convince them that we've brought it upon ourselves and were forewarned.

To test the waters and see where we may stand in a relationship, mention that we've considered taking Self Defense classes. Nonchalantly, lay some brochures around in plain view for our mates to see. No one should have a problem with us being able to defend ourselves, unless they plan on being our attacker. Stroke their ego and be persistent when asking them, "What do they think about us taking Self Defense classes?" Just look and listen for their response. Quite often, if they are abusive, they will confront us regarding the matter as soon as they've noticed the brochures.

Here, we're looking for facial expressions and body language. We're honing in on every word said and how it's said. If by chance we begin to see the sign on their forehead which reads, "I tend to get abusive," then we already know what it is.

Also, set out information in regards to acquiring a gun permit. Strike up a conversation and ask them for their thoughts regarding the matter.

Inform them that we refuse to let anyone put their hands on us. Say it with authority and study their responses.

Over or under eating because we're upset or have been beaten is Physical Abuse. Letting ourselves go, which affects our physical appearance, due to our unhappiness is Physical Abuse.

The safest way to avoid Physical Abuse is to know what we're getting ourselves into and how prepared are we to avoid it all together.

Anytime someone puts restraint or restriction on our material possessions, that's a form of Physical Abuse. At first, it may seem like it's a small matter. However, it's the abuser beginning to gain control.

For example, purposely damaging our personal belongings in an effort to keep us isolated or trapped is Physical Abuse. These are things such as: breaking our cell phones or our cars, prolonging repairs that may connect us to the outside world, or even finding no significance in having a doorbell for the outside world to reach us.

Dictating what we can wear and how we wear it is Physical Abuse. How can someone forbid us to wear what we want to wear? Our lives should be about what we like and we should never live just to please someone else more than ourselves.

In a relationship we should all try to reach a happy medium. But, if someone is telling us how we should wear our hair, and it's on our head, that's Physical Abuse.

Our style and fashion is what accents our physical appearance in the way we see fit and can afford. When the line is crossed and we cannot function freely based on our own decisions then its abusive behavior on a physical level.

The more compliance to this type of abuse only makes matters worse. It's only a matter of time before hands are being laid and it's us being abused. Do not become the power source for someone's power trip. Too many times, we'll end up saying, "We didn't think they were like that!" This is only because we didn't know how to read the writing on the wall. Even the finest print has a purpose.

Have you ever been a victim of Physical Abuse? If so, what are your plans to avoid it ever happening again?

_____

_____

_____

_____

_____

_____

_____

_____

_____

Do you have a problem with someone telling you how to where your clothes or hair?

_____

_____

_____

_____

_____

_____

Based on what you've read thus far, have you come to the realization that you were being abused and didn't realize it until things escalated?

_____

_____

_____

_____

_____

_____

_____

_____

What have you noticed that has led to you being abused that the abuser used to like about you before the relationship?

_____

_____

_____

_____

_____

_____

_____

_____

_____

What are you willing to compromise and change in order to reach a happy medium?

_____

_____

_____

_____

_____

_____

_____

_____

_____

_____

Do you feel as though it's right to stop being friends with the opposite sex to prevent a fight? Is it fair or are you the same way?

_____

_____

_____

_____

_____

_____

_____

_____

_____

_____

_____

_____

_____

_____

_____

_____

_____

_____

_____

Chapter Four

Mental Abuse – Prevention

There is nothing romantic about going into a relationship with our hearts on our sleeves. The end results could become detrimental to our health. Just like anything else in life, we normally would like to know beforehand what we are getting ourselves into. Unfortunately, most relationships are established emotionally.

The most logical practice to prepare ourselves for love is by loving ourselves, first and foremost. We have to know who we are and where we stand or we'll be vulnerable to fall for any old thing.

Do we know how a man or woman is supposed to be treated? Have we found that what we've seen as sociably accepted become the height of our expectations? Is chivalry truly dead or as a matter of fact, what is chivalry?

Mistakenly, we believe that someone else can make us happy. Yet, only we can allow joy and pain to enter and stay. Knowing our self worth is better than letting someone else determine our value.

We have to establish plans for our own lives. Then, set the level of tolerance and what is to be considered, before allowing ourselves to be thrown off course. Sometimes, there's no recovery and a life full of regret or death.

What is a mistake, and what is said or done purposely? An apology is not the cure all for all situations and circumstances. In order to have a peace of mind, we have to prevent things from being heavy on our hearts.

Here are just a few examples:

a) The first time you are called out of your name
b) The second time you're called out your name
c) Will you tolerate a second or third time to be called out your name
d) The first time you're pushed
e) The first time you're hit
f) You caught them in the act of having sex with someone else
g) Several phone numbers in their phone or strange text messages from the opposite sex
h) Same sex messages that are inappropriate or more than friendly content
i) Someone lies to you about something small such as being single or not
j) How a person makes a living
k) The other person is not keeping their word

Those were just a few examples. Tell yourself, what would bother you and to what extreme?

_____

_____

_____

_____

_____

_____

_____

_____

_____

Chapter Five

The Repeat – Prevention

The above doesn't stop until we examine the point of origin, take preventive measures, intervene, and prescribe the daily treatment for the abusers to cure themselves. To prevent the willful participation and or reoccurrence of domestic violence, continue reading and completing the exercises. Find what's for you, not what's not for you.

Chapter Six

Mental Intervention

Men, are we beginning from a position of strength or weakness?

Men, we have to begin to think our way through life and get our minds right! If not, we will continue asking ourselves, "What were we thinking?" Whoever came up with the saying, "You always hurt the one you love" is a damn fool! We know we are not worthy of starting a relationship because we can't even live up to our own expectations, let alone a woman's. Now let's deal with it!

According to Dr. Frances Cress Welsing, there are only 5 natural categories a person could be: Man, Woman, Boy, Girl and Baby. In full agreement, I believe that now we have to truthfully rethink, "Where do we stand in the entire scheme of such a thing?"

I guarantee you this: Somewhere in our lives someone robbed us of our manhood. We've been mentally ill growing up, not even knowing that we were sick in the head.

You see, if you grew up in a criminal environment, the police was known as "The Man." If you grew up in a single parent home with a woman as the head of household, then she took on the role as "The Man." If you grew up in a household who blamed another race, government or system for their failures and lack of opportunities, they were recognized as "The Man." If a person was held of high esteem because of wealth, title or position, they too were considered "The Man."

Subconsciously, from the starting gate we have been constantly trying to recapture the anticipative qualities, such as: courage, determination and vigor often thought to be appropriate to a man. Somewhere, somehow, the bar was set too high which defined manhood. Unknowingly, this caused us to feel less than, while devaluing our own self worth. Hence, we have grown physically with stagnation of the mind. We've been battling within ourselves and the world around us trying to recover from such a great loss.

This is why we look for a woman to be our girl. So she'll go to work and supply the food, clothing, and shelter. Meanwhile, we refer to her house as a crib and just hang out with our boy because in actuality we are just a baby. This is not making light of the situation at all because we're going to deal today!

Being maladjusted is to inadequately adjust to the demands and stresses of daily living. Getting straight to my point, a person's age, circumstances, support systems and temperament plays a huge role in one's perception. When abuse and violence is perceived as normalcy, it is only because abnormal behavior hasn't been identified when faced with normal circumstances.

The following is a series of questions and answers that may present some new truth. However, notice how the answers will be dramatically different from the previous discussion.

Why do men want a relationship?

Most men go into a relationship based on physical attraction, alone. We like to claim the prize, and by claiming in our minds we now possess. It's a steady stream of sex. It's "friendship" so to speak, with other motives leading back to that steady stream of sex. We've gone through puberty and women have an effect on us, like kids in a candy store. Do women mature faster than men? In this particular case, I'd agree because look at why some of us men want a relationship.

Some men go into a relationship just to have a roof over their head, which I will deal with in its entirety. There are some who begin a heterosexual relationship to hide the fact that they are homosexual.

A good catch or match made in heaven could be, a match that our family thought would be good for us based on their fondness of that person. It could be short or long term financial gain, such as she has a good job or eventually marrying into wealth.

Are men ready to give up or compromise the freedom of being single?

I will give credit where credit is due. There are a few good men. But most of us are still in the baby category at this stage in life. Remember, we have just begun to deal with our mental illness.

Our eyes and mind wander. We wander every chance we get. When a baby is hungry, a nipple is a nipple and we try to get our fill. It's the chase for many and the more women we rundown, the more of a man we claim to be and believe we are.

We justify our actions and do not believe in "What's good for the goose is good for the gander." We are more emotional than we care to admit. You see, we can cheat on a woman because we can't get pregnant and or no one is going inside of us. Our emotions control us, being that we cannot even muster the thought of the woman we're dealing with to be sexually active with another man, because "it's different."

One of the most difficult decisions in life for a man is to pick one woman to be sexually involved with. Just think about that for a minute...

There's a Strip Club fascination that takes place for some. There's clubs and bars for others. Now, even the internet is a distraction and makes it difficult to give up being single. What true fishermen doesn't like to fish? Babies and boys love to play with their friends. So, we hang out with other men and spend more time with them because that's what we do. We play house, while she's expecting us to make it a home.

Do men have time to share their lives right now or do we already find ourselves with not enough hours in a day?

A baby has all the time in the world to do nothing but play. We have a habit of being too busy to get busy. We are winging it through life pretending that we're focused. Later on though, you'll see the difference in our responses once we get our minds right.

Are men allowing a sexual/physical attraction to outweigh logical reasoning when choosing a mate?

There isn't anything logical or practical when we choose a mate. We just live the life of a wishing well. Well, we wish you say yes when we ask. We even joke around saying, "We want you to be the mother of our child." But, it never dawned on us that we would then have to be the father of said child. In a nutshell, sexual/physical attraction is the only attraction known to us while in the baby category.

Are men confusing a bed mate to a soul mate?

There is no confusion in our pursuit of happiness. Neither is there too much thought about a soul mate. A bed mate is the object of our desire. Most of us men (baby category), can't get past the thought of a woman becoming our bedmate. No matter what our age is on record, if our mind

Domestic Violence The Cure

state hasn't developed, then we're not even thinking past the present moment.

Do men have realistic goals not met yet, such as their own place to live, a car, and employment?

Many men, even in the baby category have goals set. The main goal though is sleeping with a woman. If we do have our own place, we rant and rave about it being a bachelor pad. Already, we have envisioned the many sexual encounters that we hope will take place there.

We have dreaded the times when we almost got lucky with a woman. The main reason was that we didn't have anywhere to take her to handle business. Now that we have our own place, the sky is the limit.

Most of us try to get a nice looking car, in hopes to catch a woman's attention. It seems to go hand and hand. He who has a nice car gets the nice looking woman.

Now employment and making money are two separate things. The job market nowadays is brutal. However, money is needed to buy the things we need to get attention and mask our shortcomings. The fast lane attracts many because apparently the bad boys get all the good girls. Opposites attract and there are risks taken when employment is unavailable. It's hard to convince someone to go to school when they see so many people with college degrees not working. Women become sympathetic to this and welcome us with open arms.

Are men willing to share their place, car and paycheck just for the sake of saying that they have a woman?

The majority of men (still in the baby category) wouldn't mind sharing their place with a woman. This would give them the upper hand so to speak. They are finally in a position whereas someone has to play by their rules.

Those with a car wouldn't mind sharing their car with a woman because that gives them more things to control, such as: The time, distance and frequency of usage that the woman is "allowed" to drive his car. It's an ego booster for "his" woman to be seen by others driving "his" car.

Men (baby category) are not in love with money. We are in search of power. By sharing and providing for a woman, subconsciously we have made a purchase of that person. Nonetheless, just because someone "feels" they have every right; doesn't make it right.

Do men inspect what they expect?

Not hardly! Whatever attracts a baby to a toy are the same things that attract us to women. After all, we are only playing like we are men. The way a toy looks, the size, color, sound, and functions are how we base our decisions.

Something about a woman has to catch our eye. Size matters to some, but when hopes of a sexually encounter is the underlying factor, behind closed doors, most won't discriminate. Whether she's dark or light, black or white and any shade in between, as long as she's willing, then she must be able. Depending on the conversation, meaning the words that come out of her mouth will either encourage us or discourage us.

A baby has such an imagination. For example, a toy car is designed to roll. Yet, with a creative mind, often a baby will make it fly. So, as long as we can "make" someone do as we'd like, she functions to our approval.

Can she read?

We are hardly concerned with a woman's ability to read. That would just be in our favor if she couldn't. We'd be in power to interpret life to her as we see fit, due to her inability to research the facts for herself.

Who's her family and friends?

It's hardly ever in our best of interest to know a woman's family and hope that she doesn't have many friends. A baby doesn't like to share. Our biggest fear is that her family may see right through our facade, especially a male relative. This, I believe, is why men are so protective of their daughters and female family members.

Friends cause distractions in the game we'd like to play. Perhaps, they've been through this charade themselves before and will ruin our plans.

Does she have a place, car, and visible employment?

Whether a woman has a place, car, and visible employment could go either way. If she has a place, as long as we're invited and given full reign, then it's fine. We just like to feel in charge, no matter whose name the place is in. If we have to shell out any type of money towards her place, then we automatically feel as though we have say-so.

If she has a car, we'd like to advise her on how it should be maintained. We feel as though this is our department and might not know a thing about cars. Knowledge is power, and we'd take it however it may come. If she doesn't have a car, then she could easily become our dependent.

If a woman works, we'd begin to count her money before she gets it. Many feel as though if a woman gives us her money, that's a weakness which empowers us. All that matters is we can have some or all of it. We just need control of her because we are out of control.

Would men accept a weed smoker, drinker, or casual drug user?

We are known and accused of thinking with our little head; not the head above our shoulders. Therefore, in the beginning, if a woman smokes weed but will give us sex, oh what the hell.

Alcohol has always been an enticer or excuse. There are even songs out regarding having sex and "Blame it on the alcohol!" If this drink will loosen her up to give us the big prize, then it's all good. We'd even buy it for her.

Casual drugs are too often considered soft drugs. Someone could be totally against drugs and rationalize with themselves. At first, they might look past casual drug usage because they're still getting sex. Yet, in their mind they've ruled out that this woman is a keeper. She'd be good enough to play and lay, but not good enough to stay.

It would be a match made in heaven if both people were into weed, drink, and used casual drugs. They'd never be in touch with reality because they'd both be too busy trying to escape it.

Does she belong to a church, temple, synagogue, or even have a religion?

Fornication is our big sensation. We have been known to put our own religious beliefs on the shelf for the sake of "getting some." We'd repent later if necessary. If she was into religion, we'd promise her marriage and our every intention of starting a family just to give her high hopes, while cleverly lowering her standards.

Yet, after the deed has been done, many will use religion as a form of control. A belief can easily be interpreted as how one personally sees something, regardless of how it's written. The society that we live in has been shaped this way, unfortunately. Multiple meanings of a word, also known as word-play, have always been part of the head game.

Has either of us been tested for HIV/AIDS?

Let's be totally honest. Our number one mistake is we have a visual HIV/AIDS test. We may convince ourselves that we always use a condom. But, that's still like taking a shower with our socks on. Maybe after a month, or even 6 months, of having protective sex we are ready to assume it's safe. We've been wondering for so long what the difference would be like. We may want to reproduce by now, which is just another way of staking our claim.

Everything has been going fine thus far. Our game has been playing in our favor. There's no way in hell we'd want to offend her and ask her has she been or when was the last time she's been tested for HIV/AIDS. Only a fool would talk himself out of bed, and babies don't talk that well.

Criminal Minded

With the constant rise of incarceration in America, many women will find themselves in a relationship or marriage to someone coming home from prison. This is a reality. I don't know the statistics or percentage of ex-convicts in relation to domestic violence, but I do know the game and language.

An inmate is stripped of his manhood as a form of punishment. His every move is dictated as well as restricted. Not only is he a ward of the state, he's state property. He's no longer worthy of a name and recognized by a number.

If you'd recall the 5 categories that a person could possibly be, you'll see that once in custody, Man is definitely not one of them. Being that there is no free will, our lives landslide into the Baby category. The only thing we have is our imagination.

Any prison sentence is a death sentence because our manhood is murdered. Some inmates may feel safe and secure in the role of a woman or girl while incarcerated. Many babies build bonds and refer to themselves as boys. Disastrously, they have mistaken identity based on the game and language practiced.

The greatest love letter comes from prison. This craft is perfected because unknowingly, we have connected to our feminine side. This is how we know exactly what to say to reel a woman in. We think of ourselves as the ideal man and best thing in the world for her. But we don't know we're not dealing with a full deck. We're hiding behind the mask.

When separated from the opposite sex for a significant amount of time, we may experience that our mind can play tricks on us. The constant rise in our nature reminds us that we are lacking sex. Yet, in most prisons, masturbation and any type of sexual intercourse is against the rules. Additives are added to the food to depress such a natural urge, meanwhile there are adverse effects of the mind.

Men start to resemble women, become attractive, and even preyed upon. Being gay is one thing, but to rape someone who's not a willing participant of sex is crazy. An action cannot be committed without the thought occurring first. Our body doesn't act on its' own accord. My point for mentioning this is: The minute such a thought enters the mind true masculine mindset has been depressed.

A void is about to be fulfilled three fold: First off, the baby is going to build a character for himself as the man he'd like to be. Secondly, he's in tune with his feminine side and creating what he's imagined to be a perfect relationship. Lastly, he's able to whisper the right words in an awaiting ear that's not being fulfilled.

We are attracted to the physical, yet if captured by the mental, the depth and impact of said relationship is greater. Both parties are sharing, wishing and hoping for the same things in life.

High hopes draw both of us in. The inmate would like to live up to the character he is imagining himself to be and become. The other person will base their entire future on wishful thinking. The head game controls and wins favor because the love letter has provided a service to the mind, body and soul.

How can a mere letter have such power? When doing time, there's nothing but free time to work on the image that we'd like to portray. In the free world, no one has time to articulate the exact "lines" to blow someone's mind. There's the hustle and bustle that absorbs everyone's day. Yet, while incarcerated an inmate can ration and feed just enough love through a letter which keeps someone coming back for more. Some women would rather buy hope than live life hopelessly. Remember, when a baby is hungry a nipple is a nipple. Not knowing what we're being deprived of or starving for doesn't mean starvation and deprivation does not exist.

Time invested will cause someone to become a victim without them knowing they are being victimized. As long as there's a constantly flow to feed the imagination, reality is no longer important because fantasy feels better. A woman will begin to pamper an inmate. The hardship of us doing time appears as hurt and pain. Our words of endearment are interpreted as a cry for help. Just as when a baby cries, he or she is unable to say what's wrong. Yet, the baby is picked up and showered with love to ease the pain.

Many have sincere intentions to live up to the character they have created for themselves. The best of plans are in motion. A release date is in sight and a celebration near. Throughout this entire game, sex always ends up being the grand prize. But behind the scenes, there was a language discussed amongst men full of baby talk.

Prisons are full of storytellers. There are war stories, which inmates share and glorify themselves. Many lies are told because no one is satisfied with their true selves or the way things really were.

Then there are the stories discussing relationships. Many inmates are upset because they have lost control of their significant other since they've been incarcerated. Therefore, they don't have too many nice things to say regarding women. There's a vindictive penalty that the next one must pay.

Now a woman is caring by nature. It doesn't take much to win her sympathy. Therefore, getting a visit and money order out of her is quite simple. Our sales pitch from the start is what won our first response. Ideas are exchanged and the merrymaking is perfected over time. Then here comes the realities of being released.

Halfway Houses were set up to gradually introduce inmates back into society. There are still limitations and restrictions being applied. Yet, life is no longer at a standstill and there is constant motion. If time prevails, the first chance we get is to get laid. Many don't even have the luxury of this gradual process and just are released into a cold world, hopefully to one warm embrace.

True feelings could have been developed. On the other hand, having been limited to options, was there an underlying plan all the while?

It is very difficult for someone coming out of prison to find a place to stay on their own. Society is set up to depress the supposed corrections that should have taken place during the incarceration period. With criminal back ground checks and credit checks, what is there left for a convict to do?

Beforehand, the relationship in prison had to be built. The illusion becomes so great that both would like to see it come to fruition. However, here you have two people living together that don't really know one another. Paper love can be written, yet real love has to be developed by deeds and actions in the physical form. After the heated sex begins to simmer down, reality begins to kick in.

No longer is the convict taken care of. We know that day was coming when we first received our release date. Anxiety, fear and anticipation crowded our minds. The solid plans that we thought we had instantly are derailed. How sexy and handsome we are begins to hold no weight. The Honeymoon Phase in the relationship has quickly ended. We begin to see that we are not all the man that we were cracked up to be, and so does she.

With no job, we need someone to still take care of us. Since we're free, some may begin to look at another woman as an option. Some may feel it necessary to dominate the person they are with. Having had no power in so long, forcing someone to be the ideal love of our lives stem from us not loving our own lives.

Keep in mind that we only know this perfect love on paper and perhaps through prison visits. We've both painted the perfect picture to one another. In times of discomfort, we don't really fear losing the person as much as we do the shelter. We try our best to keep the party going by alcohol, drugs and more sex. When all else fails, our minds short circuit due to lack of creativity.

It doesn't take much for a convict to act like an animal. After all, we just came out of a cage. When an animal is wounded or feels threatened, they attack, even biting the hand that feeds them. But why is it so much pain felt and the need to strike out?

When babies don't know how to properly express themselves and become overwhelmed with the inability to rectify a situation they throw a temper tantrum. This is the screaming, yelling, throwing things and hitting; identical to an abusive situation. The baby is consoled. At times women go against their better judgment just to keep the baby quiet. By giving in to demand and compromising spoils the baby and fruit of their labor. Yet, without seeing a return on their investment it's hard to let go, sort of like how a mother's love is unconditional.

If we cannot find love in our lives, we'd spend a lifetime forcing someone to become the love of our lives. It's crucial that all parties involved understand the concept of a relationship before getting into one.

Here it is, two people living together that don't really know each other. Often, there are already children present in the home. The woman has been longing for a father figure for her children. We take on the role, yet need the same nurturing that the children need because deep down we are also babies.

Pressure due to expectation makes thinking straight complex. Bad enough, we're involved with someone's children and know that we're not able to take care of our own or ourselves. This is a nagging thought that weighs us down. To feel inferior is to feel like nothing. It's hard to satisfy someone when dissatisfied with self. With something always coming up, we no longer have the time to perfect our script. In the real world the scenes change expeditiously.

I'll even play the devil's advocate: Let's say there are no children involved. However, based on the picture we've painted of ourselves and what was to take place when we got out doesn't look the same. Emotions come and go in phases and reality is always in real time.

A woman does have expectations of what's a man to do. She thought we'd give her balance. Yet, everything has been one sided. When she brings to our attention now that a refrigerator doesn't refill itself, we feel compromised because she's seeing us for who we truly are. We blame her for ruining our disguise. Yes, we may feel bad by not being able to carry our own weight around the house. But, we feel as though she has no right to let us know that we are not a man.

After all we've been through in life and just went through in prison, we feel as though she has deceived us. By her pointing out our shortcomings, we take offense and convince ourselves many things. She doesn't love us anymore. She's cheating on us. She's going to break up with us. We've lost the only one we thought that gave a damn about us. We are now licking self inflicted wounds because a baby's mind cannot comprehend adult expectancies.

Since we hurt, we want someone else to hurt. In defense, we turn her into the opposition. Her truth hurt us. Therefore, we don't care if we hurt her. Pain is pain, and vengeance is ours. How can we expect a baby to man up when he doesn't know he's a baby?

Chapter Seven

Physical Intervention

Many abusers have been arrested for domestic violence more than once. Regrettably, numerous victims have relied on a Restraining Order to change the ways of their abuser. Only to find that the abuser's violent behavior and threatening manner escalates. The majority of the time, both are caused because once in a relationship we've both failed to be self sufficient.

You see, due to the way our relationships are structured, one or the other usually cannot afford to make it on their own. This interferes with the entire intervention process. The victim hasn't healed mentally from their abusive situation. The abuser hasn't learned a lesson because no one was teaching it. Just because the rent, mortgage, and bills are due, doesn't make it okay to be back together within a month. Just because the children are crying about they miss their father, doesn't make it okay for him to come back home. Stop convincing the judge that you'd like to drop the charges for all of the wrong reasons.

The abuser and victim must get a better understanding of the significance for intervention. Being arrested, put out of the home, or forced to sleep on the couch are measures taken...but then what? We assumed this was due to doing or saying something that infringed upon the rights of the victim? Yet, how many times in our lives has this occurred, both victim and abuser, and no one told us why?

Self Control

How will someone not do something again, if they don't know why they've done it in the first place? Apologies cannot continue to be accepted if the mind is not corrected. Whatever we think is what we do. What we feel and why we feel is based on how we're thinking.

Who hasn't been under the notion that some form of possessiveness is acceptable in a relationship or marriage? If agreed, then we must understand the language and message sent to our minds. If expressing possession of a person, we agree to possess which means: to hold as property; own, occupy or dominate the mind. In turn this would make us a possessive person, which means: wanting to retain what one has, reluctant to share, jealous and domineering. In order to be domineering, we have to dominate, which is to command and or control. So, you see where I'm going with this?

Once a disastrous seed is planted in the mind, we now see the potential of toxic growth. I cannot stress it enough because we have to get this through our heads. There is no ownership in a relationship or marriage. A relationship stems from relating, not dominating. Marriage is an intimate union; combination recognized by law.

There are only two things that we must control in a relationship or marriage. One is our thoughts. Secondly, we must control our actions so they make manifest good deeds.

Self Control is when we can rise above our emotions and focus only on controlling ourselves. To have a strong feeling of love is a beautiful thing in a relationship or marriage. Yet, knowing how to deal with the emotions of fear and anger is where the damage has been done. By identifying the bad seed now, we see the fruit that it has bore or shall eventually bear.

Not just women, but everyone has the birth right called FREE WILL. Therefore, what we don't like doesn't give us the right to change someone's doing. With the screw in our heads already being loose for years, whatever we don't like blows our minds completely.

No matter how big or small an issue is that we may have, we must maintain Self Control. No one was born for us to like everything about them. Here are a few examples:

1. "I don't like the way he or she was talking to me!" So, I'll say, "Did you see whose mouth those words came out of?" That was their mouth, their thoughts, and their words. Unfortunately, you may not approve of what was said to you, but accept what you cannot control or change.

2. "I don't like the way he or she does this or that!" So, I'll say, "Did you know they have a right to act on their own accord because they are free and you don't own them?" Nowhere in life will there always be agreement, so if we can control ourselves, we can get over ourselves.

3. "I don't like the fact that he or she slept with someone else!" This is a hard pill to swallow for many. But beating the crap out of someone doesn't reverse what has occurred. With Self Control, you realize it wasn't you and it was something they decided to do out of their own free will. If you know you can't get passed this, then leave. This is the only self respecting thing a person with self control would do. Nothing or no one should motivate or dictate your actions and reactions but you.

The bottom line is, love cannot be defined or justified based on what we like. In order for balance in a relationship we're either relating or we're not. In a marriage, we're constantly striving to build and replenish intimacy or we're not.

Some may feel as though their marriage vowels obligate them to tolerate abuse because it says, "Until death do us part!" A physical death is the baby definition in reality. Anytime, in a relationship when we no longer feel alive, there is death. If we're extremely tired or unwell because of the person we're supposedly relating or married to, there is death. When our love for someone appears no longer effective and they have become totally insensitive to how their actions may make us feel, then there's death. Once our relationship or marriage causes us to lack force or vigor, there is death.

Without self control, we may never be able to determine when things have gotten out of control. It's better to recognize death than to end up dead or commit murder. Much as we'd like, the world just doesn't revolve around us. One day, we must realize that a meeting without parting is just one of life's impossibilities.

Me, Myself, and I -vs- Oppress, Depress, and Suppress

An abuser or even those with abusive traits must come to terms that, "**I** am having issues with **Myself** and need to check **Me**."

The definition of the word **oppress** is – to crush or burden by abuse of power and authority.

Men and women have placed the blame on someone and gave them power for their shortcomings in life. Therefore, the way we've been functioning has been dysfunctional. We are the only ones with the authority to be honest with ourselves. No one can see what's going on in our minds. The entire thinking process has to be overhauled.

The definition of **depress** is – to lessen the activity or strength.

A mind that has been unknowingly conditioned to deceive us by false perception or belief harbored in an adult body makes us quite vulnerable. We limit our full potential due to a mental complex that we've defectively accepted. For example, because we are different than others we lack true confidence. Anything we don't feel superb at we shy away from. We create an image and personality that shields us from the world. The way we truly feel about ourselves makes us truly weak. We long for strength yet will hide our true selves by creating a character.

Lastly, the definition of **suppress** – forcibly put to an end, prevent the development, action or expression of; restrain.

We all have work to do. Now that we're starting to understand what's going on, there are choices to be made. It's much easier to stop doing something once we understand why we do it. Without time apart to rethink our thoughts as to why we've viewed life through a dirty window pane prevents change. Not knowing why has only increased the development of an overgrown baby. As we read further, how do we suppress will be defined by the new you and I. The baby is starting to crawl...

Why Are Men And Women Insecure?

In order to establish a sound relationship, we have to be willing to leave our baggage at the door. An insecure person lacking confidence has the potential to become dangerous. What they lack will be extracted from whoever shall fall victim. They see no point in confiding in their mate. Without being able to confide in one another, there's no relating. If there's no relating, then there's no true relationship.

A guilty conscious can cause plenty of assumptions. We've seen friends, family, and couples on television being unfaithful. It could've been you and I that did a little dirt before. Nevertheless, it has settled in the back of our minds.

Supposedly, a relationship is about sharing someone's life, not dictating it. Yet, due to being insecure, we've turned possessive words into endearment. How about: handcuffing, lockdown, on smash, and you're all mine now. It's said with a smile, but literally meant. These are telltale signs of a prison being created. We begin tearing down the relationship from the very start and it becomes agonizing when growth is not in sight.

Building trust is cancelled by the lack of trust. Our definition of trust is total control. Remember, we're dealing with a mental illness and not a problem. As long as someone does what we'd like for them to do, how and when we want them to do it, that's considered trust to us. We despise suggestions and free thinking.

We have been clueless, not realizing that togetherness shouldn't restrict a person from themselves. Someone may not mind being wrapped up in our love. But, that doesn't mean smothering them. Suffocation would force anyone to gasp for air, and when we feel powerless, we try to take their breath away.

How can an insecure person bring security to a relationship? They can't, but try, not realizing that they are only in character. A common practice would be the verbal assault. The goal of this method is to make our partner weak and prone to vulnerability. Finding faults and weaknesses become our main goal. No matter what's done right, we find fault.

Keep in mind that the person we're dealing with doesn't know we're sick in the head. They're in the relationship to make the best of it. By their compliance and aim to please, they begin to confide in us to see what they can do to make us happy. That's like dropping blood around a vampire. The need for control begins to intensify. We need power and have found a source. Dominating someone by force really turns the screw that's been loose in our heads. A shake or smack eventually turns into a punch or kick. Putting them down or beating them down is a method we use to build ourselves up. Now that we're looking at it, this is crazy, and a great reason why we need time to ourselves to find ourselves.

1. Name 5 things that you are insecure about yourself and why?

_____

_____

_____

_____

_____

_____

_____

_____

_____

_____

_____

_____

_____

2. **How difficult do you find it to leave your past in the past and what baggage do you find yourself bringing into a new relationship? Why?**

_____

_____

_____

_____

_____

_____

_____

_____

_____

_____

3. **Do you feel as though someone has to earn your trust? How is your trust earned?**

_____

_____

_____

_____

_____

_____

_____

_____

_____

4. What would cause you to speculate or assume the worst about your new mate? Do you find think that what you're assuming causes an uphill battle and defeat the purpose of starting a relationship?

_____

_____

_____

_____

_____

_____

_____

_____

_____

_____

_____

5. Do you find yourself as a prisoner in your relationship or the warden? Why?

_____

_____

_____

_____

_____

_____

_____

_____

6. **Are you a controller or are you being controlled? Why or how?**

_____

_____

_____

_____

_____

_____

_____

_____

_____

_____

7. **Who's the most argumentative in your relationship? List 5 main issues that get you going and 5 main issues that get them going?**

_____

_____

_____

_____

_____

_____

_____

_____

_____

_____

_____

8. **Have you ever doubted that your relationship or marriage is never going to work, yet stay in it? Why?**

_____

_____

_____

_____

_____

_____

_____

_____

_____

_____

9. **Do you allow your support system to become a crutch for someone, only later to develop self regret?**

_____

_____

_____

_____

_____

_____

_____

_____

_____

_____

10. Do you find it impossible to leave your baggage at the door? If so, does this place the relationship at a disadvantage from the start?

_____

_____

_____

_____

_____

_____

_____

_____

_____

_____

11. How do you plan to overcome your insecurities? Until then, do you think it's fair to start a relationship knowing that you're not ready?

_____

_____

_____

_____

_____

_____

_____

_____

_____

_____

12. Has your past caused you to be defensive and over analyze someone's intentions?

_____

_____

_____

_____

_____

_____

_____

_____

_____

_____

_____

13. If you're a bitter person, why do you expect someone else to find you sweet?

_____

_____

_____

_____

_____

_____

_____

_____

_____

Chapter Eight

Verbal Abuse-Intervention

An abuser usually has to comply with a full No Contact – Restraining Order with the victim. However, this would become quite infuriating. The "Cool Down" Phase without the proper understanding makes matters worse.

How are we going to make-up with our victims, if we aren't allowed to talk to them? We'd feel as though everyone is out to ruin our relationship. We'd try calling them any way, just to have someone answer the phone and say, "Haven't we said and did enough?" hanging up, right in our ear.

Over and over the scene played out in our minds. We've massaged the method as to how we're going to apologize, overlooking why we've said or did what we've done. The key would be to stress our promise that it will never happen again. Our goal here was to convince the victims, not ourselves.

Our biggest fear is the realization that we may permanently lose the ones that we claimed to have loved. Unknowingly, we're faced to deal with another circuit overload in our mind. We aggressively want back into the relationship, before they lose complete interest in us. Yet, no time is made to focus on our own illness.

By way of reminder, when and if we do get a chance to speak with our victims, we bring up all of the good times. Using the good times to our advantage causes our victims to reminisce. More than likely the good outweighs the bad. Who wouldn't want things to be sweet like they use to? What has occurred could have happened as a first time, but doesn't mean it will be the last. There may have been previous abuse, although not frequent enough to convince the victims that the relationship or marriage is not worth the risk.

Mind manipulation can cause victims to be unaware of their circumstances. By saying all of the right things, we are dealing with the emotional side of our victims. Therefore, we are given the benefit of the doubt too fast. By interfering with their time and space to realize the predicament that they are truly in, we do both of ourselves a disservice.

1. **What are your thoughts before and now regarding a Restraining Order?**

_____

_____

_____

_____

_____

_____

_____

_____

_____

_____

_____

_____

_____

_____

2. **Do you have a different understanding about why no communication between the abuser and victim is necessary?**

_____

_____

_____

_____

_____

_____

_____

_____

3. **What was your main reason for wanting to talk to the victim or hear from the abuser?**

_____

_____

_____

_____

_____

_____

_____

_____

_____

4. Is it fair to rush back into a relationship, regardless if this was a first time abusive situation?

_____

_____

_____

_____

_____

_____

_____

_____

_____

_____

5. We may say or hear the word sorry, but does that mean that we know why things got out of hand?

_____

_____

_____

_____

_____

_____

_____

_____

_____

6. **Victim or abuser, have you ever rushed back into a relationship or marriage just to be disappointed by a reoccurrence of abuse? If so, was it based on what was said to you in the initial apology?**

_____

_____

_____

_____

_____

_____

_____

_____

_____

7. **Are you finding it better to know why things occur so that we can really change or do you expect abuse to magically disappear?**

_____

_____

_____

_____

_____

_____

_____

_____

_____

8. Did you know that a boy or girl will ask a lot of questions because they are curious to know why? They're in the need to know which prepares them to be a Man or Woman. Are you ready?

_____

_____

_____

_____

_____

_____

_____

_____

_____

_____

We Cannot Change Our Ways Until We Change Our Minds...

Chapter Nine

Redemption

Many may wonder why so many traditional things in regards to domestic violence have been omitted and how I arrived at the conclusion that Redemption is The Cure.

My objective has been to clearly demonstrate how domestic violence is actually a mental illness. It should no longer be considered as a mere behavior or attitude problem. We can no longer attribute and assign a name to every aspect of domestic violence for the sake of building text and surface curriculum. I say surface curriculum because skimming across the surface matter has only given us as follows: who, what, when, and where, while failing to give us the why. No one can change their ways, until they change their minds. If we don't know, then say we don't know!

Thus far, we've covered Prevention and Intervention. Now, let's deal with Redemption. The word redemption means an act of redeeming or atoning for a fault or mistake, or state of being redeemed. The root of redemption is to redeem, which means – do something that compensates for poor past performance or behavior. The root of redeem is deem which means to regard or consider in a specified way. Re is the prefix indicating the return to a previous condition, restoration, and withdrawal. Verbs beginning with re indicate repetition or restoration.

When we first began to deal with the Mental Intervention segment there were some undeniable points made. We keyed in on how there are only five natural categories a person could be: Man, Woman, Boy, Girl, or Baby. Also, there was stagnation of the mind because somewhere, somehow we were robbed of our manhood. Before we worry about is our relationship or marriage worth saving, we need to ask ourselves, are we worth saving? A baby cannot talk. A boy or girl can bring to someone's attention and acknowledge that they don't feel well. A man or woman will seek help and or help themselves to feel better. So, based on what we didn't know and now that we know better, it's time to do better.

The Cure

Mental

First we have to be totally honest with ourselves. We have to diagnose ourselves by discovering our every pain which leads us into a bad situation. Then we have to come up with a plan for ourselves that will strengthen us by exercising the plan.

Playtime is over, and if we're not asleep then we need to be exercising the plan. Do not engage in any activities that are not conducive with the plan. We don't need a drink to clear our heads because we know that drinking and drugs doesn't help us think better. We will no longer put ourselves in the fog; trying to see clearly. We can no longer concern ourselves with frivolous conversation nor find time to be wasted because we have work to do.

Never mind what we don't like about someone else. It's time to list things we don't like about ourselves. Only you know exactly, but here are some things that we may all relate to.

1. I am too hard on myself and would rather be like someone else. My plan to counteract this feeling is: to love the skin I'm in.

2. I feel inadequate by the things I'm not able to do, which are considered normal in other peoples' lives. My plan to counteract this is: to not only envision where I'd like to be in life, but to also plan how I'm going to get there and be on my way.

3. I point fingers and blame others for my shortcomings. My plan to counteract this is: to look out of my door every morning, and if I don't see anyone there to stop me physically, then I know I can't be stopped at all.

4. There is so much I'd like to do with myself in life but don't know how. My plan to counteract this is: to utilize the free public library and read.

5. My attitude is negative when it comes to trusting someone that I'm in a relationship with. My plan to counteract this is: to leave my baggage at the door and politely recommend they do the same.

6. I am bitter because I gave a relationship what I thought was my best and things didn't work out as expected. My plan to counteract this is: to inspect myself and come to terms with what I expect out of me. Then, if things don't work out I'll have another way to view the situation. I'll hold myself no longer at fault because someone else couldn't reciprocate to my good intentions.

7. Sometimes I get depressed because of things I don't have. My plan to counteract this is: to be thankful for what I do have and strive to obtain what I need first, rather than what I want.

8. I am a dominating person when it comes to relationships. I feel the need to dictate to make sure things go smooth, only to find out that it doesn't. My plan to counteract this is: to get it through my head that I am in charge of me and there's no ownership in a relationship or marriage.

Love is like a job because it takes work. We have the choice to love them or leave them. The above were just a few things that I discovered about myself and wanted to share with you. You'll need to ask yourself, write it down and then come up with a plan.

The Cure

Physical

Men must mean what they say and say what they mean. Remember I said, "Who ever said, you always hurt the one you love' is a damn fool." Well, I meant it. We cannot protect our loved ones if we're the ones hurting them. We have to get a grip on ourselves and only touch them with loving hands. Reckless hands come from reckless minds.

There's nothing wrong with wanting to be King of the castle. Just keep in mind that we have to be willing and able to treat them like Queens. Romance without finance truly is a nuisance. We want our relationships to be heavenly. Yet we're only accustomed to raising hell. Being "The Man" is a beautiful thing. Women will let us put them in their places, as long as we know what a pedestal is. However, we can't be "The Man" without being able to do manly things.

First of all, when dealing with the physical aspects of The Cure, here are a few pointers to keep in mind:

a) Pull your pants up because there's nothing masculine about your buttocks being exposed to the world.

b) Shower or bathe daily. Be a turn on, not a turn off.

c) Don't buy work boots for fashion costing over $100.00. Especially, if you don't have a job or plan on working in those boots to earn more than what you paid.

d) Let Air Jordan worry about his on sneakers coming out. Unless you plan on going pro. Let's invest in attire that will put us in a marketable position.

e) Poor people stay poor by trying to live like they're rich. If you're low income with hardly any income, then stay in your lane. Women admire a man of responsibility.

If we are unable to find a job, then we must create work. It may start off as something that we wouldn't want to do forever. Be mindful, it's a start. For those with felonies and have been denied by so-called Equal Opportunity Employers; know this and let's all put it in our tool boxes:

a) In order to make money, we have to come up with a plan. If we don't have a skill that is marketable, then lawful sales is where you'd want to be. Learn to buy wholesale and sell retail. Many think that it takes thousands of dollars to start a business when it doesn't. Remember, this is just a start and we have to crawl before we walk.

Example #1

It takes $15.00 to purchase a 16 0z bottle of scented body oil, and $12.00 for 48 1/3 oz roll on bottles. Do the math 16 x 3 = 48 and 48 x 5= 240. So with $27.00 you make $240 which is $213.00 profit

Example #2

Take $5.00 and buy a case of bottled water with let's say 24 bottles in a case. Make your own ice at home or borrow a cooler from someone if you don't have your own. Sell the ice cold water for $1.00. You make $24.00 which is a $19.00 profit. This is great for concerts, sporting events, and busy intersections! Save your profit to purchase a vending permit and don't look back!

Example #3

Get a lawn mower, a rake and $5.00 worth of gas. You're now officially in the lawn care business! Start with friends and neighbors who may refer you.

Example #4

If you can cut hair good, go door to door in your community and give a few samples of your work. Then charge $5.00 and you're in business. Then you save up, go to school to get licensed and then open a shop. Keep your prices affordable for the people and they will support you.

Example #5

When it snows, make sure you have a shovel ready! That's your money falling out of the sky!

Example #6

If you know how to do nails, or whatever it is you know, then what are you waiting for? Get some business cards printed up and let the world know that this is what you do. As soon as possible, register your business so that you'll be able to pay taxes on your income. By paying taxes, you then can verify your earnings.

Example #7

Who can't paint a house or room? The homeowner pays for the paint up front. All you have to do is apply it and get paid. Everyone is out to save a buck. So, whatever a person is able to pay you right now, is more than what you had sitting at home.

Example #8

Buy wholesale and buy only when you can multiply what little money you have. If you buy a dozen winter caps for $20.00 and sell them each for $5.00 that's $60.00 and a $40.00 profit. This same mathematical practice can be applied to everything we use daily in our communities: jeans, sneakers, socks, underwear, coats, jackets, jewelry, cosmetics, food, appliances, and so on.

Just because we fall down, remember the reward is in getting back up. We must stop being so eager to pay someone else attention, when we could be literally minding our own business.

It's not right for us to want to be "The Head" of the house while the body is sitting in the dark. When the bills are due, make sure we've planned on how they are going to get paid. The same couple of dollars we wasted escaping reality can now be applied and multiplied to deal with reality.

Also, pick up after ourselves, and when we see something that needs done, just do it. Only a fool would argue about the dishes piling up in the sink. A man would wash them himself if it bothers him that much. Our sole purpose for coming together should always be in the forefront of our thoughts, deeds, and actions.

Strive to learn something new every day. We don't have to become "Bob the Builder." However, there are things that a woman expects a man to know. The internet is a great tool to find things out, along with videos to demonstrate the application. All of this will raise our self esteem and prevent us from having reckless minds, which leads to reckless hands.

The Cure

Verbal

Love is work, and we have to love ourselves first. Every morning we must put on our new attitude. We check our attitudes by talking to ourselves to make sure we have on the perfect outfit for where we're trying to go today. We are quite frank with ourselves and remind ourselves that we can only be cured on a daily basis.

By reading every day and staying current with the world around us, we build vocabulary and dialogue for great conversation. Half of our arguments started because neither of us had anything to say to one another.

Let ourselves know that it's not about us and there's no "I" in "We". Self Control means to control ourselves and by the looks of things, that's plenty to keep us occupied.

It's pointless to stay in a relationship for the sake of the children. However, communication must still be proper by respecting the love once had. Just because we, as adults, break-up doesn't give either parent the right to disengage mutual rights and responsibilities. Why bad mouth one another, knowing that what we say effects the child's perception of the parent. This leads to ongoing arguments, and although we may not be trying to get back together, arguing doesn't make our minds any better.

Try to stay in real time and not too far in the past or future. How many times have we found ourselves in a full blown argument about something that neither one had the means to fulfill. Prime example, someone says that one day they'd like to go on a cruise. We may not like ships or find being in the middle of an ocean no fun. So, we open our mouths and argue about not wanting to go on a cruise. We even tell them that they're not going on a cruise either. Now remember, this is how we use to be.

Nonetheless, here's an argument that could have been avoided if we would have thought before speaking. For starters, neither one of us has money for a cruise. The key words we should have picked up on were "one day." There was no need to ruin today about something that may never happen in the future. Plus, we don't own anyone. Therefore, just because we don't want to go somewhere doesn't mean they don't have a right to go.

The Cure Exercises

If we are currently in a relationship or marriage, and things haven't gone too far as of yet, here are a few exercises that truly work:

1. Respect the walk – Respect the walk is when both parties agree to disagree and mutually understand that we need to take a walk, alone. We're not walking to cool ourselves off. We are walking to find a peace of mind. Before we lose control, we have to go find control.

No matter the time or weather, take the walk. On that walk, we talk to ourselves while thinking about what's our major malfunction. Whether it is one mile or five miles, we cannot stop walking until we've got a grip on ourselves. Life doesn't handle us; we now have a handle on our lives. Repeat, "I'm The Man" with conviction. Before long, we'll realize that our mental illness was trying to activate and we just needed a treatment to return it to a dormant state.

2. Respect the count – When we find ourselves about to react to our mental illness or even begin to feel the symptoms coming on, begin counting. We count to ourselves before speaking or doing something other than the right thing. Start counting backwards from one hundred because this causes your mind to switch its previous ill thought processing into a better state of mind.

3. Power Spot – A Power Spot is the place that we go to empower ourselves. Grab our workbooks and reflect on what we've previously told ourselves about us. Study ourselves and search for the reasons why we've become weak today. More than likely, it'll be because we've failed to follow our daily plan. We thought that just because we've been doing better it was safe to start back winging it through life.

If there has already been a separation, we must use this time apart to our advantage. Do not be in such a rush to get back together, knowing we're not ready.

1. We have an idea now as to why we do what we do. We also have a sound course of action to take. Make a daily schedule that's beneficial and stick to it like glue. This may seem crazy. But, crazy must undo what crazy has done.

2. Read on a daily basis, preferable things that will enhance our lives and make us stronger. Make sure we have an active library card and or access to the internet. Although these are the days of our lives, it's up to you and I to daily change our lives. By expanding the scope of our minds, we'll begin to view things on a grander scale.

3. Figure out why we're not ready for a relationship. Build on our weaknesses so that we re-enter or enter our relationships from a position of strength, not weakness.

4. We must ask ourselves, "Although we're not together, why are we so far apart?" Make sure we build a bridge before inviting someone to cross.

5. Unfortunately, there may come a time that we may not be getting back with the person we've abused. However, if children are involved, we still have to be a parent. Paying child support is not being a parent. Apply for Visitation Rights and be the best parent we could possibly be. That means do not question our children about: What the other parent has been up to? Who have they been dating? Who's been at their home? We have to mind our business and just

be a parent and also take care of ourselves. At the end of the day, just remember that we were the ones sick and acting a fool, not them.

Lastly, try something new before we try someone new. Find a hobby, get a pet, or just find anything constructive that will get us through the day. Tomorrow will take care of itself because it always arrives on time...

Additional Notes

_____

_____

_____

_____

_____

_____

_____

_____

_____

_____

_____

_____

_____

_____

_____

_____

_____

_____

_____

_____

_____

Order Form

Ben Official Books

710 Main Street Unit B

Middletown, CT 06457

www.benofficialbooks.com

Name: _____

Inmate ID#   _____

Address: _____

City/State   _____

		Price	
Quantity	Titles	Each	Total
_____	Domestic Violence The Cure	$15.00	_____

Shipping/Handling (Via U.S. Media Mail) $3.95 1-2

Forms Of Accepted Payments:

Certified or government issued checks and money orders, all mail in orders take 5-7 Business days to be delivered. Books can also be purchased on our website at www.benofficialbooks.com Incarcerated readers receive 25% discount, Please pay $11.25 per book and same shipping terms above apply.

www.ingramcontent.com/pod-product-compliance
Lightning Source LLC
Chambersburg PA
CBHW081155090426
42736CB00017B/3336